Whose Nose Is
This?

Wayne Lynch

Whose NOSE Is This?

Written and Photographed by
Wayne Lynch

Gareth Stevens Publishing
A WORLD ALMANAC EDUCATION GROUP COMPANY

Please visit our web site at: www.garethstevens.com
For a free color catalog describing Gareth Stevens Publishing's
list of high-quality books and multimedia programs, call
1-800-542-2595 (USA) or 1-800-387-3178 (Canada).
Gareth Stevens Publishing's fax: (414) 332-3567.

Library of Congress Cataloging-in-Publication Data

Lynch, Wayne.
    Whose nose is this? / written and photographed by Wayne Lynch.
      p. cm. — (Name that animal!)
    Includes bibliographical references and index.
    Summary: Asks the reader to identify various animals from descriptions
of their noses and provides information about the physical characteristics
and behavior of each animal.
    ISBN 0-8368-3642-1 (lib. bdg.)
    1. Nose—Juvenile literature. 2. Animals—Juvenile literature.
(1. Animals. 2. Nose.) I. Title.
QL947.L96 2003
573.8'77—dc21   2002036524

This edition first published in 2003 by
Gareth Stevens Publishing
A World Almanac Education Group Company
330 West Olive Street, Suite 100
Milwaukee, Wisconsin 53212 USA

This U.S. edition © 2003 by Gareth Stevens, Inc. Original edition © 2001
by Wayne Lynch. First published in 2001 by Whitecap Books, Vancouver.
Additional end matter © 2003 by Gareth Stevens, Inc.

Gareth Stevens series editor: Dorothy L. Gibbs
Gareth Stevens graphic designer: Katherine A. Goedheer

Printed in the United States of America

1 2 3 4 5 6 7 8 9 07 06 05 04 03

Some people have big noses. Some have small noses. But all of our noses look much the same. Our noses sneeze, sniff, and snore. They also tell us if lunch will taste good or if our sneakers need washing.

Wild animals have all kinds of different noses. Some animal noses are furry and have long whiskers. Some are big and floppy. Some are flat and scaly.

Can you name the wild animals whose noses are pictured in this book?

ike human fingerprints, the whisker spots on my upper lip are unique, which means they are different from any others. My nose is covered with scars from fighting with other animals. I am the king of beasts! I hunt animals as speedy as gazelles and as big as gnus. I attack them with my sharp claws and long teeth.

Who am I?

I am a male lion. I live in Africa and in a small part of India. I usually live in a group called a pride. A single pride has as many as forty female lions and their cubs in it. Female lions do most of the hunting. A large pride is able to protect a bigger hunting area, where there is more food.

A hunting lion sneaks up on its prey, then jumps on it. It usually kills the animal by biting its throat, so the animal cannot breathe.

The dry, scaly skin on my nose shows that I am very old. I sometimes live to be over a hundred. I use my nose to sniff out the juiciest plants to eat — even prickly cactus! Although I spend most of my time on land, I am a good swimmer. When I am tired, I like to wallow in a mud hole with other old-timers.

Who am I?

I am a giant tortoise. I live on the Galapagos Islands in the Pacific Ocean. I can weigh as much as three grown men. Because I am so large, I move very slowly. To keep blood-sucking ticks from biting through my tough, scaly skin, I let small birds eat the ticks off of me.

Mother tortoises lay eggs as big as tennis balls and bury them in deep holes to protect them until they hatch.

My sensitive nose helps me find tasty meals. I like to eat the scraps that wolves, bears, and mountain lions leave behind. I am also an excellent mouse-catcher. I can even find mice that are under snow. I listen for them with my big ears. When I hear one, I leap into the air and pin it to the ground with my front paws.

Who am I?

13

I am a red fox. I live in deserts, prairies, mountains, forests, and farmlands all across North America, Europe, and Asia. Not all red foxes have red fur. Some have black fur tipped with white. They are called silver foxes. Others have brown and tan fur. But they all belong to the red fox family.

Foxes belong to the dog family. A male fox is called a dog. A female fox is called a vixen.

My nose is big and floppy. When I snore, it jiggles. Most of the time, I live far out in the ocean, where I hunt for food. My favorite foods are fish and slippery squid. Often, I dive so deep that the water is completely black. I can hold my breath and stay underwater for over two hours.

Who am I?

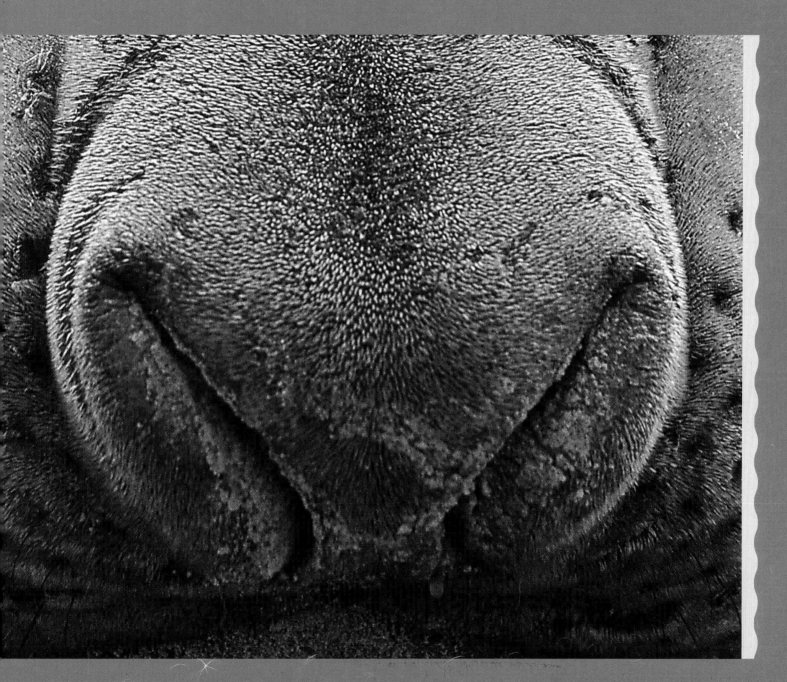

I am a male elephant seal. I live in the cold waters around Antarctica. I am the largest seal in the world. Fully grown, I am longer and heavier than a small car. Each summer, I come ashore to warm up and shed my old skin. Hundreds of us will often pack together on the same beach.

To escape a shark attack, an elephant seal will stay on the surface of the water, for only three minutes, then dive again.

Most birds cannot smell very well, but I can. When I am flying, I can easily sniff a dead animal, even if it is hidden under leaves on the forest floor. My head is bare, so food does not stick to my face very much when I eat, and I stay cleaner than most other birds. When I am hungry or angry, my red head gets redder.

Who am I?

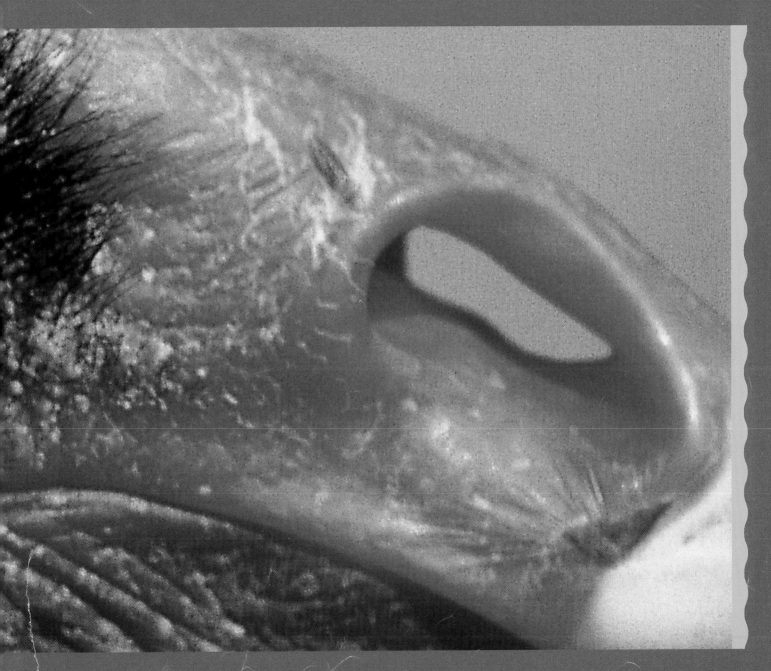

I am a turkey vulture. I live in the forests and prairies of North America and South America. I have blunt claws and weak feet, so I am not a good hunter. Instead of hunting for food, I eat animals that are already dead. I soar all day long on my large black wings, looking for food.

Turkey vultures are some of nature's best recyclers. They can eat rotting food that would make other animals sick.

I sniff twigs, leaves, and plants with my droopy, fuzzy nose, to decide if I want to eat them. In summer, I like to swim in deep lakes to escape from biting mosquitoes and blackflies. I stay cool in the water, and I can also dive for salty water lilies and other underwater plants, which are some of my favorite foods.

Who am I?

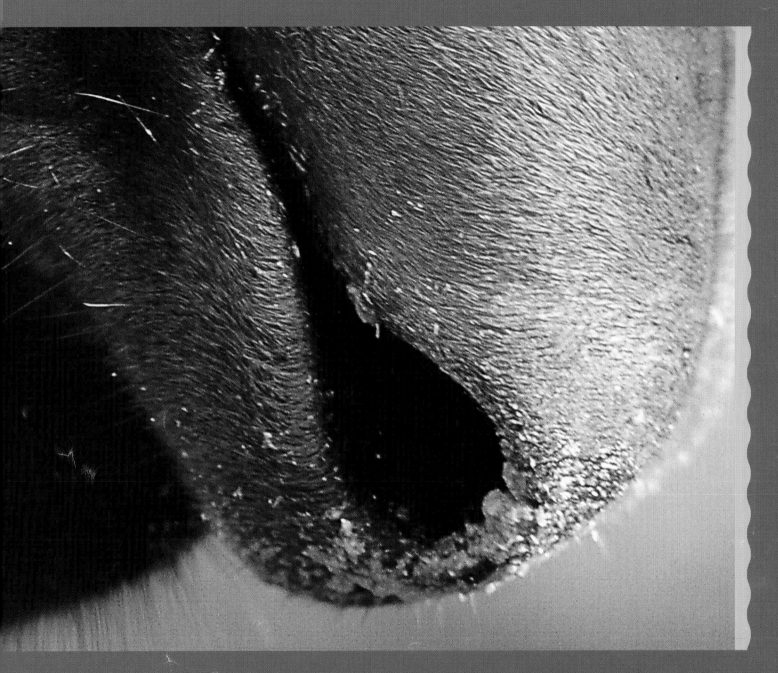

25

I am a moose. I live in the northern forests of Europe and North America. I am the largest member of the deer family. I use my long legs to wade through deep snow in winter. When hungry wolves attack me, I defend myself with my sharp front hooves.

The huge antlers on a bull moose fall off in winter, but a new set of antlers grows every summer.

I eat only eucalyptus (pronounced *you-kuh-LIP-tuhss*) leaves. They smell like cough medicine. My big, flat nose has sensitive hairs that help me find the best leaves to munch on. I eat so many that my fur smells like cough medicine, too. I spend most of my life sleeping in trees, where I am safe from wild dogs called dingoes.

Who am I?

29

I am a koala. I live in the eucalyptus forests of Australia. I am a special kind of mammal called a marsupial (pronounced *mar-soo-pee-ell*). Females like me raise our babies in a pouch we have on our bellies. My baby will stay inside my pouch until it is six months old.

After a baby koala leaves its mother's pouch, it rides on her back until it is strong enough to climb all by itself.

Index

More Books to Read

Animal Noses. Look Once, Look Again (series). David M. Schwartz (Gareth Stevens)

Knowing about Noses. Allan Fowler (Children's Press)

Noses That Plow and Poke. Diane Swanson (Greystone Books)

Whose Nose Is This: A Look at Beaks, Snouts, and Trunks. Peg Hall (Picture Window Books)

Concord
South Side